FOLK

BOOKS BY JACOB McARTHUR MOONEY

The New Layman's Almanac (2008)
Folk (2011)

FOLK

POEMS

Jacob McArthur Mooney

McClelland & Stewart

Library and Archives Canada Cataloguing in Publication

Mooney, Jacob McArthur
Folk / Jacob McArthur Mooney.

Poems.

ISBN 978-0-7710-5939-1

I. Title.

PS8626.O5928F65 2011   C811.'6   C2010-904532-7

Library of Congress Control Number: 2010940062

We acknowledge the financial support of the Government of Canada through the
Book Publishing Industry Development Program and that of the Government of Ontario
through the Ontario Media Development Corporation's Ontario Book Initiative. We further
acknowledge the support of the Canada Council for the Arts and the Ontario Arts Council
for our publishing program.

Typeset in Centaur by M&S, Toronto
Printed and bound in Canada

This book was produced using ancient-forest friendly papers.

McClelland & Stewart Ltd.
75 Sherbourne Street
Toronto, Ontario
M5A 2P9
www.mcclelland.com

1 2 3 4 5   15 14 13 12 11

He looked me in the eye but didn't say a thing, just turned redder.

"Your brother shot Miko with the poor fucker's own gun, Nick. The fucking gun he won at your big poker game. You know the game I mean, don't you Nick? Maybe your remember that last hand especially. And the funny things that can happen when you start hanging too long with the wrong people.... So now, what you're gonna do is set up a meeting between your brother and me. Someday you'll both thank me for saving you from a life of punishment and regret."

He stuffed his hand in the pockets of his sharply-creased slacks. "I don't understand what it is we have to fear, Keith. For all his faults, my brother can be clever at business. He has great skill at protecting himself."

"You know as well as I do that with that kind of a load—that size—there will always be someone out there to claim it. And those kind of guys have guns and money—and lawyers, too, probably. All of which can get you killed. Just do what I tell you and you'll live to rip off another day."

He didn't answer. He looked for a second like he was going to make a break for somewhere or something. I kicked out the toe of my work boot and a display cabinet full of little silver boxes exploded in a shower of glass.

"Easy now, Keith, easy now. Come on now. Maybe I should call the cops."

"You call the cops? Give me a fucking break. Suppose I tell them about all the illegal pharmaceuticals you got stashed in the back of that old pharmacy you bought last month over in

FOLK

An Introduction to the Geographer's Love Song of His Life

You and I were born on an impossible island.
Local folklore purported that when seen by The Gods
the island drew a perfect circle in the sea.
Trained skeptics set out to disprove this superstition.
First they counted paces, then somebody invented
a device that could properly validate their findings.
Someone elsewhere was launched into space.
Evidence came down from international committees
suggesting that the island was not quite a circle.
There were irregular masses stretching out into the ocean.

This forever sabotaged the national psychology.
Revisions were brokered for The National Flag.
Parliament discussed renaming the island, from *Reglatug,*
which in our language meant *circle,* to *Reatikus,*
which in our language meant *here.*
A revolution spread westward and defeated these ideas.
Men were killed for using the new name in a song.
The Ph.D.s who preceded me were made to use protractors,
watched over by a soldier who covered his face.

But you and I were born in the decades of forgetting.
The priestess told us at our wedding
that our grandfathers were generals, and had fought
on opposite sides of The War. After their campaigns,
order was restored to our capital city. We took
our first-born daughter there so she could see
the graveyards. We buried our legs in the sand.

The summer I found work at The National Academy
they uncovered latent metals in the silt of our lakebeds.
All this and proper planning brought the island new prosperity.
Refugees from other islands aimed their boats at our beaches
while we took that little house on the shoreline I had promised.
You saw it in the background of a bicycle commercial.
We made love for the first time in sixteen years, while outside
the sounds we made in coupling were lost inside the waves.

We both voted for the man who promised us modernity,
attended speeches that were heard on every island in the chain.
The year I got ill at the family reunion, he set about the task
of rendering the circle. Fill from poorer islands
was lifted in by planes. Crowds gathered at the pier
to watch the workmen smooth the edges, brought roses
for their wives and fresh breakfast every shift.
Our largest corporations paid the ancillary costs.
Old colleagues from my college days engineered the dig.
The young man we voted for was voted in again.

In the fifth year of the digging I lost my sense of sight.
I sat in my deck chair and listened to the workers.
Our cities were congested by counter-demonstrations.
Certain elements complained that the work was too expensive,
that some of our birdlife would be lost to the project.
The year we bought the walker they finished the circle,
shot a man into space to bring back photographic proof.
The book of his life story has been adapted into film.
You keep it in the living room and read to me at bedtime.
The shoreline has since been moved far away.
In the lonely afternoons I sing towards the waves:
Oh, my voice! My people-voice! Come find me!

FOLK ONE:
IN THE VECTOR FIELD

St. Margaret's Bay, 1998–99

There was nothing to associate the individual.

DR. JOHN BUTT, *former chief coroner*
of Nova Scotia, January 1999

The Ocean Sings of Incendiary Things

To begin with, it was beautiful.

     A solar flare. A break
     in the beacon-speak of lights.
          All seabirds and sailors
     blinked in perfect unison. From chutzpah
     into flail, from hum
     into sizzle crash,
     the come-apart
     was counterpunch, the wheeze
     of pressurized air was heraldry,
          a droop
     in the fuselage
     that focuses the heart.

Now come marauder, come meal,
be erected in their honour.

Come reducer, sob-machine, emperor
of sulk and sunlit private moments.

Reckoner. Decision. Come sprinkle your storyboards
across their country notions. The friendliness exhibit zeroes in.

They'll see parts of you in beaver dams, pocket lint,
school lunches. Come berate their histrionics. But before that,

come be heard. Be soluble, smothered,
pulled apart and pummelled clean.

Come retrieve your beauty. I believe
in beauty, in the
wish-thin
packaging
and pander of the word.

THIS SPACE RESERVED FOR THE NAMES AND ADDRESSES OF VICTIMS

Name: _____ Address: _____ Marginalia:

(prime

pre-ironic
development
space)

The Vector Field

So now the world is coming
with its cameras to document,
to register an audience, to blur away our
hard-scrubbed
homogeneity, our
hardiness, our
hardness.

Everyone can tell you where they were
when the world arrived. Everybody happened
to be walking their dog,
eyes on the ocean, 11
P.M. and raining.

Those who didn't own dogs
went out walking their intentions.

Everyone can illustrate
the actions of the airplane
in the seconds before impact. A
roll, a
twist. A
wing bent across its face like a
feign, a
faint, a
knowing inward breath.

We spent the next three weeks
discussing windows. Every cracked window in every
eastward-facing pane
was a witness. *It passed through us.* Drunk husbands
and accidental breaks were recast,

                                              their perspectives were flattened
in the neighbours' rushed retellings. And everyone wanted
to pause for their portrait. Everyone wanted
to figure.

TWO THEORIES OF THE IMPACT

I

                       That the problem
first burrowed in unbroken underwater,
minus the wings and other
peripherals unsuited to
the shift in local gravity. The pressure differential
drew a plan for its attack, then kicked out
the windows, stippled down the vessel's length
along its opened pores.
                        Thereafter certain objects
could see where they stood, and the sudden
cartoon logic forced the interloper open
at its seams, then at its
seams' seams. Down this insurrection,
the breaking gained momentum and surprised
the unbreakable — a bolt, its head
shorn free from the shaft,

a crumpled medal found inside
a crevice carved from bone.

An air bubble burping at the surface.
An oil slick.

And six or seven seagulls
squawking through the din.

That at a certain speed
the salt in ocean water coalesces into concrete.
At a certain speed, spun momentum can
churn objects into dust,

dust that embraces itself
as it deathrolls down the sky.

This is why
they never found a piece of the wreckage too heavy
to be hauled from the water by hand. Most of it
escaped microscopic,

lifted on the wind
and carried, a cloud,
blind, towards the shore. We call this theory
Immediate Translation.

And it predicts
that the first island in
will get infamous.

So no Mounties but still,
one morning that winter,
a man we all knew

woke up,
shot his two young sons in
their sleep, shuffled back
to tell the wife,

the shotgun's languid afterbirth
folding smoke into the carpet.

The wife has moved to the mainland.
She hangs out with the hairdressers, making
conversation. She'll catch the young sailors
as they try to slink away, hold their scared new
heads in her hands. *You look good, kid.*
> *Handsome.*
> *Everybody's at their best today.*

Deterministic Error Chain

Some people
went downright crazy. Or rather, some people, with
crazy at the ready, moved onto the empathetic surfaces
offered by the impact, let it peek through their crazy like
a theme, a thick volume, placed under them for height.

                                          Like

the woman
whose dog tweezed free a human hand from the beach
and half-buried it out back. She dug herself
a dozen test holes, certain she was living on some lost
Mi'kmaq gravesite. She ended up attracting questions. *No, sir,*
I can't imagine why I'd want to kill somebody.

                                        Or

the man
who misplaced six months in inventory
of first chapters from the Bookmobile's
fiction section. He burned plastic in the hearth.
Quit his job fixing cars. Was sad.

                                Or

those of us
who gave up flight. Or those who've since surrendered flight
to a sense of the miraculous, muse aloud
on backlit landings, hold their breath and look straight down.

                                        Or

the mayors
of the peripheral communities
who got in line for funding made available
to all those considering a permanent memorial.

Or

the kid
who saw the sign at the saltwater pool that read
No Diving and thought, *I should really draw a picture
of an airplane, there.*

STATION AND VICINITY

Every night in winter
a forgotten million snowflakes fall
on the ocean and so all
they learn about is water.

The headland bends to its tides,
the tides to the peninsula's
geographic lapses, and the populace
kneads geography
into something it can use.

Even their number, 400, is a kind
of a home. A series of split decisions.

The plane came down
to make good on all our pessimisms, its
        efficient package
more than half the town's 400
stencilled faint between other
invisible markers:
        longitude and
        latitude, the local borders huddled
        in the skin of hand-drawn maps.

Gravity owes us nothing.
The debris slipped lost
behind the surface cover. Someone sent in
instruments to measure the circle's severity, dug up

corporate histories, a list of enemies
for everyone on board.

The rescue efforts narrowed
from panic to a second panic better handled
by preconceived instruction. Men arrived to sink
        the deputized rescuers'
boots into the mud so as to hold them there,
        in place.

All witnesses were listed by centre
and perimeter:
        several shadowed tracts of beach,
        and what they noticed when they stretched themselves
        as far as they could reach.

DEAD RECKONING

for Ettore Bellini and Alessandro Tosi

In the days before radar
paths were plotted through the sky along
celestial relations: down the long snake
cinched across the tightened belt, from
the water bearer's left to right arm.

In the daytime they looked down,
memorized the passive vacillations of our rivers,
the polygons imposed on forests by towns. Long voyages
relied on straighter lines. Twenty-two degrees forever east
equalled Europe. Twenty-three and you'd be lost
to the ocean's open mouth. Know your place.

Train the plane to recognize itself
as planned performance, tracking its momentum
in clean footprints through the sky.

Spend your landlocked nights taking survey:
where were the stars and where are they now?
Their shimmering is their only regular report, each outdated
crest of light says, *I existed. At least I was there
to beam myself towards you.*
                              Changes come as exclamations
                              like a siren or
a foot against the door. Things haven't been the same
for centuries, now. The bank is coming in the morning

for the house. I didn't know how to tell you so I waited around
for that which wasn't there
to show itself in something
inconceivable that was.

SIN OF OMISSION

The priest
was Haitian and unpopular, sent
from Halifax to lift the
church's sinking numbers.
Someone made a joke about
      colonialism.
Someone made a joke about
how he choked on certain words:
    roshery, Simmeritin,
    Good instead of *God.*
He liked his vestments arranged
in a reliable order, would
reach for them blindly, one
finger in his scripture.
He had me come in early
to heat and light the room, dust
the Christ-bearing frames
of the Passion. On the Sunday
of the crash, he
decided not to mention it, just
Those people
in the ocean, those people
are not us.

Songs for the Cool Kids in Towns without Traffic Lights

Those who arrived with graduate degrees
ready to lie fallow on the land and fashioned subdivisions
out of dormant fields.

Those who could speak with some detachment about
the famous local facial features
imported from Europe and left
to fester through centuries
        of stubborn
interbreeding. *Notice the pronounced zygomatic arches
and the straightened, simian jaw line.*

Those who looked in from the periphery
of raucous public meetings, who voted every time
but never saw a single leftist get elected.

Those whose children grew up in the back rows
of civics classes, who slouched in tourist coffee shops shone on
by cable TV. Who bought imported music and
couldn't believe their bad luck when
        (for all their practised nonchalance)
the visiting media
        (whose names they knew)
would always pull from the crowd
the most toothless
                authenticity available
to pester with questions engineered
to pinch the face of the catastrophe.

Yessir, I'll talk awhile. Are you here to ask about my zygomatic arches?

IRISH

In that semester of the airplane
we started learning genealogy. I remember
being disappointed that
my ancestors weren't aristocrats, that they
traced themselves through Europe
as ghosts of ethnohistory; part of the crowd in
the crowd scene. Lost within the lithographed
trajectory of battles
so thick they bent the borders
of other nations at their hinges. Attack.
Defence. A pause to allow
the cartographers their survey.
The date labelled bold in the bottom
left-hand corner. And all the normal
New World escape routes: New York, Chicago, the
Mississippi, the
St. Lawrence. What is it
we hope for when we ask about
our histories?
            (A picture frame.)
A map of the world with our bodies
as equator. As
meridian. As
mirror.

A mourner met me on the sidewalk
the week of the memorial. Told me
he thinks he has

Canadian roots, like that's something
that exists. I dug out
a recently retired two-dollar bill.
They don't make these anymore.
Have it.

He put it in his pocket,
let it lead him down the street.

POLAROID OF A LIVING ROOM IN LUNENBURG COUNTY
SINCE FEATURED IN A DISCOUNT POSTCARD

The secret of this house is that it's dirty.

Beyond the straight lines and
binary design schemes,
the undersides of objects bear
notices of life, fingerprint-shaped stains left
by things without fingerprints (candleholders,
shoes, plants pushed in their pots six inches
to the left).

In the den a dog and cat
are accompanied by what
their insertions indicate
(unashamed allegiance,
practised sensuality). Shed slivers
of their costumes   twist
into the carpet. Vacuuming just presses in the hair.

At the window,
no dandruff has gathered to dance or be deposited.
The furniture assumes a stoic pose. It's a captured negation
of time's forward progress, the story of the light along the walls.

The secret of this house is sediment. Accumulation. Antiques
from all different eras.

On the wall – a calendar.
Another portrait of a landscape
held fast within a frame.

Do you think it's possible two hundred people could fly
from one Centre of International Trade to another and,
if something (hypothetically)

                        happened to their airplane,
none of their deaths would be a blessing
to the world as a whole?

                        Don't answer that.
If you do it's either a conspiracy or evidence

                        that one of us is wasting
                        the other person's time.

Sphere of Influence

Every name printed in the paper, Abideau
to Ziegler, and a younger friend asked, *Is that the order that
they died in?* I said, *No, it's just
the alphabet.*

But what if both were true? Seatmates, exchanging
business bylines over Maine, arrive at
strange relationships: Shulter, Singer, Smucker. *Wait.*

The coincidence
breaks over them and rains throughout
the cabin. The aircraft tilts
the action eastward to announce its
true intentions:

> *The dead are coming
> to be folded into integers. They are here
> to be your culture. They'll be here
> inside the night.*

Newsprint on my hands.
Disowned names smudged free and left to float
to foreign surfaces. A pen. A desk. The greying tape at the handle
of my Little League bat. Death gets into things like that.

The total losses were left
for the Feds to figure out.

The total losses included
the given names of future loss.

A Surface Normal (Five Points in the Life of a Wave)

1. No Slope
The reporter kicks a stone up to face
the coming ocean, double takes at the ground
as if just now, six days in,
she's noticed Nova Scotia
curled in the space made cool by
her shadow, stabbed
by buttered stilts
that lift at her heel, grace
her weight.
          The geographic angle is abandoned inside
her fourth
          abdominal breath: after time, velocity,
body counts, and the empty
Injured column.

2. Up Slope
The setting of a bare-staged play is mentioned
in the playwright's bio as *This place*
I grew up in. This place
of empty spaces. All I can remember is the air.

3. No Slope
An intermission. A blink in the vigil's
passive record. The camera crew packs up for editing and

the crowd that had gathered gathers its thoughts.

4. *Down Slope*

That October, on the fourteenth floor
of a brand-new building that I swear
was somehow haunted, I toss a penny off the balcony
and lose it in the jet stream. True story.

5. *Flat Slope*

Blurry, either
from fog or TV static: ten private paramedics
parked along the shore. Lights on. Arcs extending eastward
to the rumoured point of entry. *These locals know enough*
to not expect survivors.

                      But their beams build a registry
of every wave's arrival. Seats and things
returned to utility
by their weightlessness and shape.

How far were you willing to come
by car? The airline offered freebies
and your brain shuffled back
to its assurances: *It is x times more likely*
to die by lightning than by flight. Still, you thought,
No thank you and invested in an atlas.

                                      Check in at
the inn. Meet the fishermen who set out
in search of the survivors. Meet their kids.

Go speak to the women, they know idioms.
They'll make you dinner that requires
eight pots to prepare. Blend your brown passport
into the scenery
and stand beside the lighthouse where
you watched the people stand.

When someone asks you your relation
to the lost say,
                Brother.
When they check your name against
their list say,
                -in-Law.
When they question your intentions,
hold up your St. Christopher and wait for
signs of storm.
                Grief
is not composed of grief. Grief

is a compulsion. Walk up to the dead
and lay your body on their bodies
until you share a central chill.

SHELTER

We are standing on the deck
that no one stands on.

There's evidence of drizzle
on everything but us: the snare drum rattle of
a beer can on the lawn, the neighbour's retriever
backed so tight under their eaves
he looks like a spot on the wall
left unpainted.

We ponder, unencumbered, eyes
on the sky — an airplane's wake,
four clouds, the sun.

You say my hands are warm, so I focus
on the physics of transference. My palm: your fingers.
Your fingers: my wrist. My boots,

darker
in the canopy's shadow.

With these,
I once stepped ankle-deep
in the ocean.

No water broke the seal.
No waves complained.

Asshole with a Shotgun

Cue the rediscovery of ridicule
and blame. The first local story
once the plane began to fade
was the kid who got bit
in the jaw by a dog.
                        I remember
invading the property of the welder who owned her
the length of that whole summer no one knew
was born to be a lead-in. A hand pressed flat
against his bleached siding. *One one-thousand,*
two one-thousand.
                        A firecracker
hot with our intentions in the middle
of his yard. He came out, half-dressed,
let the shotgun win the argument
pulled voiceless between us.

The dog bawled out from deep inside
the trailer's windows, pawing at the cracks
in the glass.
                        Its eventual attack
allowed for conversations on the news about new worries.
Child endangerment versus
the right to love an animal. Speakers slouched into the story
for two exhausted evenings, but all I can remember is
that asshole with the shotgun, cheap
swagger in his legs and purple women
inked across both shoulders.

We forget that things aren't usually related
in the intimate ways we remember.
There was no plane ablaze in the hemlock overhead.
The soil didn't shudder as he slammed his screen door.
The dog's ashes weren't scattered in the ocean
or mixed into the sand of public beaches.

The man who read the news gave up the exposé bravely.
We turn again, now, to the ongoing disaster.

We face what we've been following
and pick up where we left it.

Signage Prompt

Cue the rediscovery of artifice
and range. The first major party of that school year centred
on a fog-mounted bungalow
three metres
from the shore.
            I remember you driving
with your chin against the wheel
tuned to every hiccup in the road.

How much did the deer need to cross
before it found us? A curious foot
through the wild and into
a New World with our litter left
as fungal introductions,
                then up the unsupportive
pile to where pebbles
became gravel without learning either name. Finally,
she vaulted an invisible divider
into our concretion of directions, our
terrain. She entered our sightlines
weakened, submissive,
lost in some long country where
she didn't speak the language. First contact with our armour
stopped her heart and left hyperbole
up to the antenna that split her at the neck.

We tracked her back
through the skid of fur and bowel failure, found
her head, upright, thinking thoughts
for the ditch. Then her ears. The doll's eyes. The sticky red
bit of her tongue. *I never killed anything
this big before,* you said. I sat down and
put my hand in something wet.
Two eyes of coloured light appeared
and swung themselves towards us, brightening the scene
as you went back to find your phone. Their invasion paused
            against your deconstructed Audi, drew
lines behind our bodies to suffer us with plot. And then
her torso. A mosquito. One entire lumberyard
            of trees shadowed backwards
onto a black curtain with a tear along its seam.

Twenty-Seven Socialists in the Kitchen, and Some Cows

They were mascots of the housewarming
that month at a friend's place,
a rental made cheap by its placement between
two prime dairy pastures. Four times a day
the cows played through, bumping their back engines
on the mailbox, leaving
manure like waterlogged reminders every divot.

Witless infiltrators to our loud-as-fuck escape, needing
six months of solid exercise before
passing as 400-lb gorillas in the room, before
even slipping through the ancient frames.

An electric fiddle led selections
from *Our Country Kitchen*
and later *The People's Handbook of Song*. Choruses
were lifted through the thin and warping walls, answered by
the bathroom dweller's stuttered stomps and howls
until all you heard were choruses,
chortled or falsetto.
                              Heads thrown back
in public unison, a drink
spilled on the upswing every 36 bars.

The teenage population took their bargained-down
beer supply (2.2 bottles allotted per head)
out into the backyard and challenged all the cattle
to a pickup game of tag. Arguments surfaced

about how small you'd need to be
to effectively ride on a cow.

Later, with the headspins, we lay in a
safe patch, head to gut to head to gut to head. Beasts
burdened past us, a flick of a tail and a line drawn curved
against the stars. *Analka, Sky-Bovine.* Voices
cambered outwards, topical
and hushed. *Somebody, sometime's,*
gonna write a book about all this.
I never saw the rednecks
so proud before last week. It's important,
I think, to not say anything more than,
It's a tragedy. More than,
Hey,
what can anybody
do?

IMPERIAL

It's our fault we built ourselves
so indivisible and soft, a gloss along the landscape
one molecule thick. The plaques we built onto our buildings
were bitter and illegible. Under dust and ancient typefaces
they weathered their predictions, said
Airplane, said
Rebranding, said
Don't Take Your Names for Granted.

We deserved what came
to render us its afterthought. Our public faces
pressed the land into a photo
of the land that we locked
inside a frame. Our houses in their poses. Our posted
histories. Forty-seven facts about life in former times.

What could we build
that would have withstood
such a shockwave as the one
the plane became? How many coats of white paint
on our walls would it take
to stand up to its demands, its
forced redistributions?

Two photos of a lighthouse set square on fading newsprint.
A lighthouse.   A lighthouse.
        The eye, adrift,
looking for the differences
crouched between the two.

Mr. Meticulous Teaches Us a Lesson in Bravery

for Vic Gerden

A wave flattens out for a flicker at its apex,
an unplaceable blip of no-slope. So short

       its very naming
is a hyphen-branch to its history.

       We lose it again
before we finish with the word.

       Men set out with science to establish
       the precise moment of the plane's
       recommitment to the surface. Minute,
       second, parts of the second so thin
       they reach out from the uncountable
       to appear in the problem as wind conditions,
       as the tension in the pilot's right hand.

Men set out in mid-September,
came home with salt stains on their gloves.

Then they sold their houses.
Sprawled out into the country like cracks.

To a Skittish Flyer on the Subject of Civil Engineering

There's a dude here who tells me he studies engineering,
says *Civil. What's civil?* I ask.

So he points to the row of closed doors in the alcove
tight behind the cockpit's eyes and nose. *That.*

Stacks of plastic stretched on our ambitions, the idea that forced
explosions could somehow be relaxing.

Civil means movement=0, he says. *Static stuff: railways, buildings,
roads.* Its input here is illusion, then.

Decorations on mass to the speed of light squared, how a fly
can navigate inside a speeding car and not be squished flat

by the bigger picture. The dude is listing all the objects
in the hatch overhead: *elastics, masks, thirty feet*

of coloured cordage. Even this phone's been folded
into the envelope of motion, magnets to lock it in place

during takeoff. But don't worry, now. I'll go. This is costing
more per minute than I make in half an hour. Say hello to home

for me. Take care.

THE EARTH IS FLAT: SIX TRIANGULATIONS ON THE IMPACT SITE

> "The three sites combined — Whalesback, Bayswater, and the
> actual crash site — make a triangular shape, which is reflected
> in the design of the memorials."
>
> *(Shared text found on the interpretative panels*
> *erected at both major Swissair 111 memorials.)*

1. Eastward, from the Aspotogan

Rent a boat and set off from the closest
setting-off point. A peninsula designed
to delineate two bays,
to present a captive home
for a winding rural road. Run the motor
                    until
the waves cut your momentum
and the trees on the shoreline
blur away to branchless green.

If you meet another pleasure craft
idle in that nondescript
zero on the ocean, don't ask her why she's there.
She'll extend the same
courtesy to you. Look away or pretend to
                    look away towards the town.

2. North, from the Departure Gate

They drew this plan in the days when Transatlantic
meant stopping at the last
continental land mass to refuel. So a European trip starts north
and bends on Viking memory towards
a tangent of
the curvature of
Earth. You can't see how this makes sense unless
you look at it from space. Like how
a hydrophobic child will run up and down the shoreline
testing every depth before deciding on the shallowest
reference point to jump from. One hand
on the sand. One hand
stretching forward. A pause to face the target, then
a push. Gliding on inertia and
the body-lock of dread.

3. West, from Cape Sable

Vanguard. Bellwether. Introductory
island. A hyphen tying
the world to its ends. Hydras
for the Flat Earth and waves so high
they forget you in the trough.

Drop something off
the mainland and the current will deliver it
towards this open bracket
            stretched to catch whatever
we have lost in transportation.

One day a whole crate
of cotton shirts. A twin engine ascended from
the airstrip to return them.
        To finish
the cycle
        we started.

4. Up, from the Ocean Floor

Step one: Feed the bottom dwellers.
            Use whatever has arrived from higher worlds.

Step two: Catch the bottom dwellers.
            It's simple – they are stupid and have no sense of sight.

Step three: Prepare the bottom dwellers.
            They cook up easy. They've grown soft on fatty foods.

Step four: Serve the bottom dwellers.
            Serve them to the mourners at emotive public meals.

Step five: Clean your knives.
            Consider the consumed.

5. Down, from the Bigger Picture

Look down on the rescue ships
idle on the water, the meniscus insects
perched on its skin. Look

for signs of intention. A slow ride home suggests
no luck. Speed says survival. Keep tabs.

Inflect our maps
with diacritical marks. A little hermeneutical
oomph for our flatlands, our bleached and
bordered homes.

This is where we are,
and by *where*, we mean *who*, our
party in the function. Our
scope. Our
score. Look inside our
sphere at the
calligraphy of air, the
silent orchestration, the
hypertext, flow.

6. *South, from the City*

A day in town for shopping with a
friend's trusting family. A treatise on
the subject of
The Military Grid.

Friend said, *They're all the
same exact size. The trip around each block takes the
same amount of time.* I asked for proof
so we lined up on either side
of the street and (of course)

took off sprinting once certain
we'd made it to unseen. I lapped around
a simple square but
Friend caught an unmarked
public park and spent the morning
getting found. I remember pulling up
at the Start/Finish line, alkaline tongue
and heaving torso attempting
to downwash the heat wave.

I followed the walkers
upstream with my eyes, witnessed them
turn the distant corner and never reappear.

I wrapped my legs around a park bench.
Gripped the Bus Stop sign for safety.

WATERFOLK

That our geography is give-and-take. Untraceable
and never easy. That the ocean invades

every sign of weakness; it flits through a sprawl of sand
or threads through loose rock. A colony of lake

at the last resolution. Fingers reached around from
the next embedded world. A cradle of thin and frigid

embraces. Fjord. Strandline. That we border the whole planet
in the passive tense. Node of harbour. Current schematics.

The sun. The last Appalachian son. That every summer home
they ever built along the shore was built with its back to the rest.

That whatever comes for us must carry its own gravity.
That our quiet is unnatural. A hushing of the tides.

JETSTREAMFOLK

That we have continental relatives we never even met but who
lay claim to us with whispers, with rumours of smog that

no one takes the blame for. That every wind is either
background noise or outlaw, a neutered neutral party or

outlier to the curve. That the urge to venture seaward is
suggested in the heavens. That our provincial bird and flower

never chose us as their patrons, never looked down
on our shy faces and fell headlong into swoon.

That we maybe never swept our ecosystem off its feet.
That these species only landed where their gliding gave them up.

That the pulse of solidarity we wanted may have wanted
the exact same harbourage from us.

CRASHFOLK

That skin is soft. And stretchable for miles.
That the new bones we built inside ourselves

are not the antidotes we hoped for. That we can never win.
Even when we float unconcerned across the decades.

Even if we serve dinner on the trip. We believe in all mortalities
displayed in public spaces. Fear of fire. Fear of flight. L'avion dit,

Un Calligramme! bends herself around us and burrows
through the soil, infusing into every crop and weed. Come down

and build your crater-wake. We will be your
death mask. That wasn't our intention when we built our

homes and roads, but it sure was our intention when we
slept inside the sky.

NAMESFOLK

That the words that pull things free also bind them
to their ancestry. An air corridor. A stream for jets. The

mnemonic world waits for you to trip into its story. That every
sense of danger is just instinct learning when and how

to interrupt your thoughts and curve against your voice box.
That our history books are essential texts, but not

to the study of history. Flashbulb psychophysics narrow
their wide eyes to this: that the patterns we've been hoping for

are not the payoff. The payoff is in pacing off your own backyard
and then accusing the neighbours of infringing on your land.

I'm not suggesting this to lessen the impact of the losses.
I'm asking what has nested in the scar of their retreat.

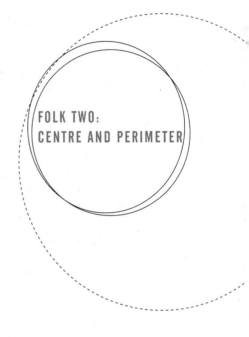

FOLK TWO:
CENTRE AND PERIMETER

Malton, 2008–09

Everybody's scared of this place
(and staying away).
Your little house on Memory Lane.
ELLIOTT SMITH, *"Memory Lane"*

AIRPORT AND DERRY

The plane parades

over the park, then the college, then a knife's shadow on flatware
off the grey sheath around my Mississauga map.

There be dragons.

Trail guides — I'm learning to tell time by the night sky,
Northeastern headed south, 9:30. YYZ — JFK —

GVA. Have fun.

The terminal building abandons her brood, but I can't
help waving. I will be their scale key. They'll be my

carrier pigeons.

Twin engine flares light the neighbourhood's west boundary:
Seattle, Montreal, Boston — Send. More. Bookstores.

The saddest parts of cities

seem to settle around their airports. Echo-
location and pattern recognition.

In the fifties they expanded

this peripheral strip and changed its name. You can see it now
from space. I hear the din wriggle in through thin night air.

Hum and Ber:

the takeoff and the shake it makes. Radar sings the view
of my new neighbours in the darkness, channelling vibrations

through their rental.

Bleary-eyed émigrés get pushed against the brick. *Feel,*
it's got rhythm. This means we're living everywhere. Hum

and Ber, also

Hub and Home. Also Hiding
and Hopeful and Here.

CENTRE AND PERIMETER

A small boy with a cello. Two Sikhs on red bicycles. An-
other. Forty/forty – Grits and Tories. Enough small town for years.

Our masala-hot sun melts the Toronto template,
shifts boundaries and blinds the windows of my nation-house.

Welcome to the festival of dignified reserve.
Civil service code words spark out from circled holes.

Hunter orange is easy for the nightshift to see. *Sewer Lane.*
Rain Drainage. Three metres to drop. The road team overtimes on.

Whatever they're mining must be
rooted in deep, six-foot piles of dirt on the sidewalk.

Unearthing is framed as a form of retrieval,
but it's Malton's only act of creation. What results, The Unearth,

gets pounded into pavement. Or
we build our houses from it, whole streets from other people's

hand-me-down histories. This asphalt is trilingual.
Walk it, feel its lumps in your spine. Everything is everyone else.

THE FIRST WAVE OF MALTON HOUSING UNITS FAIL

It begins with believing
your warped and weakened houses want the best for you despite
their bad intestines. Their guttural melodies
burping through the night. Problem plumbing. Poor cement.
Houses erected to lend credence to the headlines
harnessed to the land. *The Development Story.*
The Immigration Angle. Assemble your complaints
from *i*'s gone undotted, from the *t*'s left to find a line
to lean themselves against. A door
curves towards its frame but never closes. A faucet winces
and intones to you its whistle, saying,
Nothing is alright behind these walls.
The sedentary functions
of sloped foundations fester
deep into the inventory left to us by landscape.

What is it they say about
the damage done by water?
                It's terminal. Once it worms inside of you
it turns to take down. An invader from
the slow, unplanning earth.

DARCEL AND MORNING STAR

At lunch, the Lincoln kids
stake positions in the library. Boys dressed
as U.S. Army snipers stage
empty-baggie deals to fluster public librarians.

One block in all directions, convenience stores
with unlicensed meat counters
renew the pig in non-Western ways — the tongue, the kidneys:
in the heart of the animal
there's colour. Almost
                              sound.
In the square, the same pigeon's been run over
twelve times, every squeaky curve of him
rolled flat — except one leg, arrowed upward by its break.
D of E tracking bracelet beaming radio bleats to the Bird Gods.
Inside, well-secured PCs perch on Gates Foundation
stations. Men appear from doors disguised as walls.
          The ESL class is given forty minutes, most
browse the stock of Disney distractions, mouth the names
of authors on the new arrivals shelf. I borrow old movies
and four-dollar thrillers by the bagful, print poetry
                    off the machines that
sound like something chewing on bone. Hood up. Music on.
                              Growl the day out.
Back against the metal detector doormen, I tease out
the readable parts of bad papers. There's a war on. A race.
Two kids in Toronto are sentenced as adults,
          now we're allowed

their eighth-grade victim's name.

        His name is Rage Ghost. His name is Weight.

By one, the sniper boys are gone.
A sign advocating breast exams is missing.

AIRPORT AND JETLINER

Clear customs

and stand up. The streets are standing
with you. Go outside and meet the buses
in their concrete birth canal, bordered
in every way by road.

This permanence lends shape to the air that falls around us.

Anything cyclical
will understand migration. If only we lived beside the ocean I'd
show you — whole stories in the muscle memory tied to its reach.
Entire archeologies in every inward breath.

There used to be more
declarative entrances. At Pier 21 in Halifax
they've commissioned a museum and supplied every building
with artists who
host open houses
through the cruise ship season. I'd take it anytime

over this.
Take the Mississauga Transit route seven, north or south.
It passes by the airport. Sit up front
and watch the driver give directions.

No.
That's east of here.
Go stand by the Coke machine, they'll find you.
They'll find you.
Okay.
Okay.

The Sikh man in the second row
has been there every time I've ridden.

He acts as a reference
if you're setting a coordinate,
one more point of worship
in this edifice perpetually
stretching in all dimensions.

RIDDLES FOR LESTER B. PEARSON INTERNATIONAL AIRPORT

after Mary Dalton

The utmost altar
of the technocrat religion. Believe in me.
You'll have to. Wait and I'll wink you
onto land.

Constellations dissolve
on the order of my echo.

Marco —   Polo —
I welcomed you down in every dark.

*

A retrofitted prop from a
cartoon fantasy, lacking the machine that
applies hat, jacket, combs your hair,
inserts breakfast.

If you ride my clenched teeth,
I'll feed you to the future.

Always watch that last step. The earth will want
to reassert a slower speed. Allow it.

*

Dream navigation doesn't need
a sense of physics. Come above and get lost
by the schedule. Report to the clouds. Report
on the weather: one ambitious pigeon
climbing skyward in the wind, a plastic bag
skidding to a stop on the runway.

Geese intercepting
a distant visit's future path.

I'm imperial. Impatient. I perch. I foresee.

✢

You come to me protected
by fear and my formalities,
super-conscious of the couple
of unmarked candy bars
ticking away inside your bag.

Cloistered in my leap-between, everyone
is nationless. Everyone's a nation.

Everyone has something to declare.

AIRPORT AND RIPON

On Airport, they stack the plazas
high on bad foundations, four adjoining jewellers
hold up offices, apartments
that break bylaws by hiding
behind the walls of butcher shops.

Down the road, The Last Grill, the last
white-owned business, bides its time until
the churches close on Sunday, spilling their communities
(incommunicado) out
into the street.

The walls harbour thirty years
of Leafs' memorabilia
but the old man who cooks
keeps the TV on La Liga.

I bring all this up to my waitress, who smiles, says,
Five jewellers. The fifth sign says
diamonds in Punjabi.

And what's the point of central planning
if everyone's ambitious? I ask
if she's ambitious. She
blushes, takes the tip.

Moodie and Moodie

1. The Outer Edge

Cul-de-sac people don't need anybody.

Cul-de-sac people like talking to themselves,
staying inside to watch the grass burn. The engine of invention
for window tint, television,
the privacy plant, home school. Bad citizens are
the best kind of people, the hardest
to own.
        Their afterthought roads grow like loopholes, like
        lakes. Commuter clutches so thick the sound
        can't pass, gets lost in insulation, in the gaps

                                  between

                                  waves.

2. The Inner Edge

Mohammed lives on Moodie with his dad and his dad's dad.

They complain about the rent, the latenightedness
of neighbours. Grandpa's got no legs, lost them
on the job. Now he watches home movies,
falls asleep on the sofa smelling of dust and

old cheese. They sit in the crosswind on Sundays discussing
                politics and cricket, wearing
                one another's clothes. Not needing
                anybody, just talking
                to themselves.

Mark Makes Friends with the Cultists Down the Road

You would have known better if you weren't eighteen,
weren't so recently arrived from Aurora. You'd have known
the only business an old white man and an Island woman
could have with each other in this neighbourhood is God.

You accepted every packet, hung up their hyperbole and
rapture on the wall. You started a collection, offered them a seat.
Filed away flyers and old *Maxims* to make room for their gestures,
their list of open-ended questions. I came out and said hello

in my derogatory meter. The woman smiled like she knew
I was collecting for a poem. You're a natural apostle for the end
of the world, booster of the perfect fits fostered by conspiracy.
You cornered me in our common kitchen to explain the NAU.

You had dark and earnest reasons for harbouring a rifle, kept your
gun club membership on permanent display. They came back
that afternoon you left us to go home, it was up to me to tell them.
They seemed to understand and didn't ask me about Jesus.

One of us offered up a handshake and a shrug. This is how
we closed your show, your winking curiosity. What
do you know now, Mark, that you didn't know before?
What parts of you are better off for asking?

From Here You'll Have to Work Your Way Around It

Then what else would you rather have define you?
        Things intersect. They do.

What lines would you draw in the scatterpoint?
        Things intersect. They do.

✻

For one afternoon in the week before
Remembrance Day, the kids from Sawy Preschool brought
charcoal to the graveyard, rubbed out impressions
of Christian symbology, alien names like
Le Marchant, Coliacovo, Hughes. Things intersect.

They do. The marking stones host leaf pile lean-tos,
bright with held moisture like the morning
I slipped spread-eagle in my driveway.
I have no name for this building
I rent the western half of,
I still can't find its edges, its

innocent X and Y.

✻

So what else would you rather have define you?
    Things intersect. They do.

What histories do the sidewalks know?
    Things intersect. They do.

  *

Here be monuments:
    The bones they found while digging the subway.
    Frozen holes that had once bedded street signs.
    Prayer beads dropped in an S on the asphalt.
    The olive bread turns. The garbage around it.
    On the day I moved in – three dark hairs
                     in the dew on my window
                  that I mistook for cracks.
    Directories. Parking lots. Public bathrooms. Lines. Things

intersect. They do. My *there*, your *after*. My *house*, your *home*.
I caught a mouse eating through the
plaster between us. Neighbour, will you help me drive it out?
All species need a niche in their ecosystems. Things intersect,

    they do.

    All geography requires
    is a faith in repetition
    and for things to intersect.

    They do.

Monica and Brandon Gate

February opened on two frozen birds.

I spent the month walking past them, beside
the telephone line that had failed to provide
a permanent fix, that released their claws
from its rubber axle
and swung them, sleeping,
down onto the sidewalk. Nobody
talked about the birds.
Crowds that gathered for the buses didn't
talk about the birds.

An old man paused
to consider their position, fat breasts bloated
by the thaws that go unnoticed
in deep winter, caught between storms
and the nighttime's whistled siege.
The old man looked up at me and grimaced because –
Did you know this? – it's impossible
to encounter something dead at your bus stop
and maintain a grimaceless face.

I didn't pick them up but
I did keep up a diary. *February 8th*: Birds turned over
by the wind or some dog. None of the blood
I expected. *February 12th*: Smaller bird kicked ten feet
down the curb, one wing thrown forward
stopped it from rolling. Beak chipped. No blood. *February*

22nd: Another snowfall and the sidewalks ploughed.
Two perfect circles left untouched around each body.
No footprints in the snow. No salt.

*

The next week the birds were both gone.

Someone posted an opinion. *It's not right the city
didn't do something sooner. This shit's
a health risk. We're all in this together,
remember?* The sign attracted insults: *Busybody, Crazy
Bitch,* three words pulled from a language I can't read.
The sign was taken down
and replaced by an improvement:
five lines of packing tape preserving it from vandals.

The weather waned that March,
folded back the snow to show
a whole city of dead birds,
slumped forward on their silence like
a growth of cheap new houses. Seventeen in the skate park
alone. Four found in the gravel that had gathered
by the sewer drain. Two mailed to the guy
who handles sanitation, thawing in the cardboard box
his secretary worried was a bomb.

LEESBURG AND TEESWATER

Our churches have altered their service times
to coincide with the Airport Authority's shifts:

Our Lady of the Cross on Morning Star.
Our Lady of the Airwaves on York.

Our Lady of Clumsy Hate Speech
at the corners of the last Irish streets.

Our Lady of *Do You See Us? We're Speaking to Each Other
and There Are Other Fearful Miracles We Hope to Overturn.*

I went to mass last Sunday. I used to go more often. I once went

>   to a wedding and yawned with poor timing, walked in on
>   two waiters having sex at the reception, sat
>   with ice cubes in my pockets until
>   taken home on the assumption I'd pissed myself.

>   I went to funerals to get lost in Father's
>   metaphors. Words begat the burials.
>   They filled the first spaces over death.

>   I went to special services:
>   days marking the end of certain indignities,
>   days assigned to Saints, days when the minutes would
>   dam themselves against me,
>   days when the biblical passages quoted could

only be explained through the lens of civic outrage
over the allowing of gays in the army, for example, or
the election of an atheist to the school board.

I went to normal services
and assisted at the altar. All I retained was the weight
of the sounds in my mouth: rosary, benef-
icence, homily, chalice. That and
the knowledge
of when to sit and stand.

I went to mass last Sunday. I used to go quite often.

This was the first time
no one had to make me, the first time freed
by the knack for non-belief.

MY ADVICE IS TO BELIEVE IN POETRY AND NOTHING

for Paul Vermeersch

Let's pretend it's summer, eat ice cream
in the fog. I've lost the sense of question
I've expected of the city, so let's go
to where it isn't and
trace around its shape.

A blind man and his dog took the stairs at Union Station,
thought things over for no seconds on the lip between
the subway and the ledge. I yakked in your toilet
this morning with the shower on. It tore a hole inside
my throat and broke blood vessels in both eyes. The island
has a zoo and we could try to name the birds. I can't
be much for animals, I wrote the draft of this poem
in a leather-bound notebook.

There's two points of observation in the middle of the island,
straddling the village full of yuppies that complain about
the airport. This is the one blunt difference between people:
those who'd make a study of the lake versus
those who'd enlist the city's skyline. Get yourself
uncomfortable. On one side of the postcard:
tower and geometry. On the other side:
all three hundred names for blue.

And it's as sad to be unsure
as it is to know too well
which side of the display was made for you.

Diversionary Landing

The French accident arrived as panic
banished from the fog. It bounced twice
along the asphalt and
collapsed into our gully, head against
the city limits.

A ripcord of smoke at the runway's end.
The lit tip of a paramedic's dropped cigarette.

The pilot took the slide, arrived at the mic:
Your topographical maps looked like bull's eyes to me. Plus
your eyes were distracting, with all that looking up.
Each fixated pair two flares inside their sockets.

Someone said it was a miracle
that nobody was killed,
threw a tarp over the Airbus and
started on the survey.

The soil found under
her impact scar said *nature.*
If not *natural,* at least its shy
ancestral root.

The dirt that found the fuselage
and muddied the water
of high-pressure hoses
was the one thing on the property

not taken by invention, in no way coveted or
grounded into thought.

TWILIGHT AND WOODGREEN

Head to the dirt I spot dropped footprints
in the flattened bike trail through the woods:
baggie, matchstick, roach. Repeat. These canopy curtains.
            These co-conspirators.

These secret-brokers glow in the day's
first revolution. Call it lightdrop, dawning, go,
go. Our neighbourhood feeds itself with veins built
            from boot steps.

This one grows from the temple to
the shopping mall. Desire lines:
try to do one-third of all your walking on the grass.
            Your original thoughts are shortcuts.

Make the cartographers' guild
aware of this sedition, they'd
love to draw someplace new and say you haven't
            been there, that you're therefore

less perceptive. Wrong —
you've been somewhere twice
once you return to it at night, and they're yet to do
            a map all in black.

By seven the sun has sprawled itself
clear across Toronto, dropped in on all
the same places. We night civilians hurry home
            to beat the rising –

the 24-hour McDonald's kids on shift change,
the Woodbine winners, the losers with blisters
and holes in their shoes, the high-school drug king,
            the bat watcher,

        a man I've never met who sits down
        in the daybreak, offers me a cigarette,
        asks to read the lines in my hand.

6:30 A.M. —
Such abandon in the pace the night
takes into daybreak. Two kids in the back of a Honda
insisting:
>   *Hold-your-breath-and-here-we-go-*
>   *now-make-a-wish-okay-we-did-it.*

Below them, something cowers
in the crook of the city, arms over ears to the
                        sound of traffic
checked cautious by fog, the reports of
a collapse in Quebec. He stretches out to fill his shelter
made of concrete, charity blankets, the back of an old
election sign, that irony.
                        Finch Street
drums on above him, channelled through
the asphalt, the
pads of my feet.

The cleanup committee's anti-graffiti
swoop of red paint
runs the frost-lacquered whole of the support beam.

                        Overpass.
                        Passover.

A mark.
To save his house.

6:32 A.M. —
Such abandon in the pace the night
takes into daybreak. Two kids in the back of a Honda
insisting:

> *Look-up-we'll-sing-the-names-*
> *of-all-the-pictures-in-the-stars.*

This is home.

Or, this
is the place where I'm staying.
But what else would you rather have define you?
This is where we live, it's what
grows up around us.

Half-moon in the autumn
like an eyelash. This is exactly what I need to step away from.
Also: economies of scale, loss expressed
as physics, all poetry written by landlords.
This is the smell of our neighbourhood: dogs,
cumin, wine in the punt of its bottle, awaiting transportation
on a hot night with strong wind.
This is historiography, the stopping and restarting
of segregated clocks.
Then what else would you rather have defined?
This is it. I can speak to you of objects, but never
The Objective. I'd draw a circle around our known world if
it didn't mean unveiling
an unknown one as well.
This is a very old problem with circles.

Go for a walk in the dark by yourself.
Go for three days without speaking.
This is your country, a colony of polished,
uninhabited shelves. As no one trusts the word *nation* anymore,

we're happy to be living without it.
       This isn't patriotism. Maybe it's the opposite,
the decision to
bend with the wind.

From Here You'll Have to Make It Up Yourself

for Mike Snow, and St. Christopher

What sinkhole would offer the best home for your fall?
The first lesson in possession is learning your name.

What forms of ownership are the easiest to fake?
The first lesson in possession is learning your name.

*

I went to Easter service
at the church with coloured glass. No one looked up
to lock eyes with the engravings. A man cut the grass
and laid the sound through our acoustics.
     No one thought to ask me
     how I thought the earth was made.
It ended early so I crossed
the highway to the park. Several pigeons with bad wings
dreamt of taking flight to follow. True story.

*

What is it you're hoping will want to drop on top of you?
The first lesson in possession is learning your name.

What forms of ownership are the easiest to fake?
The first lesson in possession is learning your name.

*

A short list of unclaimed patronages:
    Existential remorse. Survivor's
    mythology. Tides. Motion
    sensing. The recently
    unearthed. Those who used invention
    to pay homage to their heroes:

Einsteinium,   The first lesson in
Callicebus aureipalati,   possession is
the Galilean Moons.   the learning of your name.

The first step in our departure was identifying nature.
    Come here, your name is Nature. Then *You*
    will be History, and *Your name is*
    Possession. All three of you, while dancing,
    will be Home.

PRIVACY AND SPRAWL

1.
I just dreamt recovery.
An ocean scene centred
on a brightly painted boat. Not sure if I was any
of the bodies recovered. It's been said in a dream
you are everything you see.

2.
I just dreamt that mail was erotic,
that reach was not something you command but instead
some magnetic
                hand-to-hand instinct, constant between bodies
that have burnt the same hair, between
skin that has sweat a shared warmth.

3.
I just dreamt about an ocean. It refused to say its name.

4.
I just dreamt about collapse. Some incalculable weight
in the bedroom, suffocation. I just dreamt myself to death.
I woke up belly-down, gravity and fantasy feeling out
the argument, the air
in my water glass breaking its bubble
and, in doing so, surfacing, returning home unspoken for.

5.
I just dreamt that an airplane had landed
in the park across the street, that nobody recognized
the people who stepped out of it.

That the flag of their country
was branded on their chests.

6.
I just dreamt about design. (I'm the kind of atheist
who thinks he'll win the lotto.)

7.
I just dreamt of a lightning strike
shaped like a hand.
It left me dry and
exothermic in the night.

The couple from the corner store
found me in the morning,
dragged me to their house, painted
greens into my eyes where
the impact shocked them white.

Found me a chair and taught me
their language. Sang me gently
into morning, made me tell them
all my names. Made me dance.

8.

I just dreamt of veiled engine sounds (a cat
purring, a rockslide, the rumble of an
overloaded dryer). Wake up, we'll go outside and watch
the Red Eye climb, yell goodbyes, cupped hands to
perfect voices.

              These streets mean
property. Their exits mean
I love you. It's been said in a dream
you see everything you've seen.

Eleven years and we approach
our final losses: the groundfish industry, that intimate shift
wherein a new adult comes to understand the certainty
of death in his own lifetime. Not even death but
the *ceasing-to-exist* effect. The rented casket. Every trip
on the subway shuffles daydreams:
a bomb or
The Bomb or
a two-train collision and in such a tight space, what would
become of that momentum? How deep inside each other
would the lead cars drill? Would rescuers
arrive at either end to find the front seats
reborn beyond the flames? An explosion
and suddenly there's prophecies
of train blown out the sewer drain
at some minor intersection surprised to learn
it's been on the line this whole time.

Eleven years and what remembers? A memorial attended
by precisely sixteen mourners. Acknowledgement
on the ten o'clock news. Two photos of a lighthouse
on the back page of some paper. Changes
to the laws that govern onboard entertainment.
       Two hundred
and twenty-nine people. Again: two hundred
twenty-
nine, two
hun-

dred twen-
ty-nine, t
wo hun
d r
e   d & twe

nt

     y-

          n

i

          n

     e people
     died. And.

THE EARTH IS ROUND: SIX APPROACHES TO MALTON, ONTARIO

1. Northbound, from the Lakeshore

The city's centrepiece is
not a building
   or a borough
    {ouroboros}

It's not the ocean
but just as endless to the swimmer.

It's one of those rare holy places
where the surface slips from your memory

and the notion of a great and contiguous planet
requires faith
   or a dive tank. Every large lake
   has stories about sea monsters. Every
   large lake but ours.

2. Westward, from the City

Twenty-one stops from my brother's house on the Danforth
to Islington. Then the MT 11 to the mall.
Get on at a quarter to or after. There's music on the radio –
   The Blues.
The driver's name is Dave. Sometimes Bill. Three cans
of Dr. Pepper and a St. Christopher medal
form an altar to his tape-framed licence.

The walk's not far. Run home and the wind will strengthen at
the intersections. If you know the basic route,

you can get there going blind.

Fold your hands in your lap on the bus. Cross your legs.
Put your hood up. Be as many concentric circles
as you can until your stop.

3. Up, from the Spiny Recesses of Hell

This woman lives at our GO stop. I came down one Sunday
neck-deep in a book. She wedged in past the pages, stated,
No trains today, son. Just buses. You didn't see the sign?
I swore at her through the holes between my teeth,
started up the naked stairs, turned and saw her face
pressed flush against the glass
like an extinct butterfly, like
something found floating
in a bucket of rain.

I'm a good person.

I once gave her a dollar and polite conversation.
I thought it was Monday. I had exact fare.

4. Eastward, from the Outer Suburbs

The harvest lasted some four hundred
straight seasons, bales of self-sufficient towns sucked up
by the whirligig urban unfoundry. Erindale. Cooksville.

It takes a village.

It takes another.

Where there used to be neighbourhoods
there's Electoral Divisions choked on hyphens. Hydras.
Every little outpost
                but ours
has a Welcome Sign, written in a classical script.

Someone stole the *Malton*, but the authorities are on it.
                It remains, until then, unfound.
The city wants to wait before ordering another,
                been waiting since 1991.

5. South, from the Farming Lines

Start: First Line —
        Second Line —
        Third Line —
        Fourth Line —
        Fifth Line —
                :Left turn.

[All adventures are illogical. It's worth exploring down an unlit
sideroad, just to see the congress where they all come together. Every
corner is empty. Have a cigarette. Take a piss. Crank the radio — The
Blues. Nobody is watching you sing.]

6. *Down, from the Universe*
    for N.B. (atheist)

You'll need a flat place. I know one.
You'll need a wide angle, the kind of creation myth
    that says you are small and that
    everything lasts forever.
You'll need a car, maybe. Or one of those trains that run off into
    the country. Something to resist the wind. Five dollars.
You'll need company, someone you can talk to who knows how
    our roads work, can wave off commuters enraged on bagels
    and sippy-cup coffee. *I'm free Sunday night.*
A warm coat. Maybe. An umbrella if it's summer. Maybe
    you'll bring something from home. A bright number
    in imported colours that doesn't know you've left.
    Nothing goofy or effeminate – there be rednecks
    way out here.
Sit on the corner by the cornfields. Wait until there's no cars.
Are you ready? I'll need my camera. Four exposures.
The intersection waits for you to walk into its centre.
From a flat part of the planet, you can look in all directions
    and know that, eventually, you're always looking home.
And beyond home, always looking at yourself, staring off.
    Like the moment where the seventh day slides into the first.
    Like the snake that swallows its tail.

MAPFOLK

That the sports team I like best is the most morally defensible,
and the same goes for the country I live in. Fill in the photograph

with agriculture, politics. Unfold the shrinking circles
and have someone tell Greenland the news.

But this imagining is only a comfort to those
born sponsored in its vertices, while a fissure-bleed

of rural routes reigns out its unpaved ripple. Tell me everything:
guess your home against the globe, mark your height

along the wall. Step onto a compass rose centred in a public square
that identifies the distances to sixteen major cities. Break a piece

off your body and bury it to root. Grow an army of witnesses
to walk out all the measurements. Double check everybody's math.

That the wilderness was not supplanted by our planning. It's
always important to know where you stand. That we raised our

tame ambitions straight up through their strata. That
things are born from other things, there's heredity in objects

built stiff into their fabric. Ask an arsonist or shaman to
give smoke another name. Every hour, on the hour, point north.

That we are trained to see in transfers, the shift in plastic's afterlife
where it's shrugged, discarded, to be pondered as imposter.

Where east runs dry on the surface of a globe and resets its
intentions to The West. Like the heart's rehearsal of its secret

final wink. A hand on your shoulder. A letter in your hand.
Delta world. River world. Stream of steam and seam of sea.

EMPIREFOLK

That we have a choice of waiting kin who'd do anything
for family. Bend themselves over logic or the rules, sell the house

to be a sponsor. A patriarch. A patron. Play the name game nightly
as you thread yourself home. Follow streets and their labels from

foreign to familiar, mouth the mantras on their indexed parade
across your glass. That we still take note of the discoverers of laws

that kept timeless vigil for eternities before us. Electricity. Orbit.
We remember that somebody discovered them their names.

That this might be how rapture works, lacking the dramatics
of fire or redemption, everyone suddenly forgets their name.

You could build something there, beyond ownership and thought.
Drive us home through the darkness to the darkness and stay.

VECTORFIELDFOLK

"Everything that has ever been called 'Folk Art' has always
reflected domination."

— *Theodor Adorno*

Source and sink. That each association gleaned
is just the spherical allowing us a peek inside its head.

That no one made us ready for the speed the earth was moving,
something kept us sheltered from the spin. That there are

ancillary lives on the surfaces of solids, a Coriolis Effect
to the tragedy patterns. That we can claim homes without knowing

the birthplace of the lumber that plays hostess to our story, the
species of grass seeds scattered on the lawn. Map the air around

the wingspan, pull the wind into a sock. We can study
and be honest. We can opt for better answers:

humanism, Godlessness. We can loop our finer points into
a brainwave to replay them, but the Where of us will always win.

FLIGHT LOG: NOTES

Folk One:

Swissair Flight 111 went down on September 2, 1998, in St. Margaret's
Bay, Nova Scotia. With an official death toll of 229, the Swissair
disaster ranks as the twentieth most deadly incident in aviation history.

In its original context, the quote from the former Chief Coroner
Dr. John Butt that begins "Folk One" refers to the difficulty in
ascertaining individual IDs from the partial human remains found
at the Swissair 111 crash site. Dr. Butt was quoted by journalist
Nancy Robb in her story entitled "229 people, 15,000 body parts;
pathologists help solve Swissair 111's grisly puzzles," which appeared in
the *Canadian Medical Association Journal* 160 (2): January 26, 1999.

Several poems in this first section began as riffs on individual images
from the song "Desolation Row" by Bob Dylan. It was first recorded
on August 5, 1965, and was featured on Dylan's sixth studio album,
Highway 61 Revisited. While most allusions have been edited out in
rewrites, the debt the poems owe to the song remains.

Folk Two:

Malton, Ontario, is a neighbourhood in the northeast corner of
Mississauga, bordered by Toronto to the east and Brampton to the
north. Traditionally a community of working-class immigrants,
the area has, in the past, been home to relocated populations from
Poland, England, Jamaica, and Ireland. Malton is now predominantly

a South Asian and Middle Eastern neighbourhood. The community's chief employer is Lester B. Pearson International Airport (formerly the Malton Airport), the busiest airport in Canada.

The epigraph to "Folk Two" is from Elliott Smith's posthumous 2004 album *From a Basement on the Hill* (ANTI-Records). Most textual sources list the second selected line as either "and they're staying away" or "they're staying away." However, aural evidence from both the studio version and live recordings would suggest that Smith sang the song as it is remembered here.

The suite of Mary Dalton riddles that inspired "Riddles for Lester B. Pearson International Airport" is called "I'm Bursting to Tell: Riddles for Conception Bay." It appeared in her collection *Red Ledger* (Véhicule Press, 2006).

Mike Snow, to whom "From Here You'll Have to Make It Up Alone" is dedicated, is the current name of Michail Itkis, the former CEO of a company called Interactive Flight Technologies. That company's on-board entertainment system is the prime suspect in the investigation into the fire aboard Flight 111. The fact that Mr. Itkis changed his name does not necessarily imply any guilt, of course. It is not always helpful to have villains.

The species *Callicebus aureipalatii*, referenced in "From Here You'll Have to Make It Up Alone," translates as "monkey of the golden palace." The naming rights to this species were purchased by the Montreal-based Internet gambling website GoldenPalace.com. The common English name for the species is now "GoldenPalace.com Monkey."

The title of "My Advice Is to Believe in Poetry and Nothing" is inspired by a line in "Inside Gus" by Al Purdy, a poem written for his friend Ralph Gustafson and published in *The Stone Bird* (McClelland & Stewart, 1981).

The Theodor Adorno quote that acts as an epigraph to the final poem is from his 1974 monograph, *Minima Moralia: Reflections from Damaged Life.*

This book is not an act of journalism. I moved things around. I made stuff up.

ACKNOWLEDGEMENTS

This book's preparation was supported by the Canada Council for the Arts through their Grants to Professional Writers Program.

Some of these poems had previously appeared in the following journals and magazines: *All Rights Reserved, Canadian Notes & Queries, CV2, Horizon, Misunderstandings Magazine, My Favorite Bullet, The Ottawa Arts Review, The Puritan, The Walrus,* and *Zygote in My Coffee.*

"An Introduction to the Geographer's Love Song of His Life" was included in the chapbook *Vox Populism* published by The Emergency Response Unit (Toronto) in 2010.

I'd like to thank everyone at the University of Guelph's MFA Program in Creative Writing. This book, and all future books, is better because I was a part of their community.

I would also like to thank the loose assemblage of Toronto poets who formed the informal workshopping group "The Roaming Poetry Death Squad" beginning in 2007.

I am indebted to the following peers and teachers for their attention to these poems: Ken Babstock, Dionne Brand, Karen Houle, Jeff Latosik, Dennis Lee, Michael Lista, Sandy Pool, Steven Rowe, Paul Vermeersch, and the late, great Constance Rooke. It's good to have people.

I'm also indebted to the team at McClelland & Stewart Ltd., which includes Anita Chong, Ellen Seligman, Ruta Liormonas, and my editor, Stan Dragland.